What's the Deal with Retirement Planning for Women?

By

MARCIA A. MANTELL

R∃THINK PRESS

First published in the USA in 2015 by People Tested

This edition published in 2019 by Rethink Press (www.rethinkpress.com)

Cover image © Shutterstock | mareandmare/Lina Truman

Author portrait by Leise Jones Photography

For Dan, Katie and Lindsay

Remembering all those long hours in the car
talking about retirement

Contents

Introduction 7

Is "Retirement" Just About the Money? 9

How Much Will I Need for Retirement? 15

Why is Retirement Different for Women? 23

How Big Is Your "Freedom Fund"? 31

Why Is Shoe Shopping Important for
     Your Retirement? 43

Remember "Because I Said So!"? 51

Do I Have to Worry About Saving for Retirement if I
     Have a Pension Plan/a Husband/My House Is
     Paid Off? (Or Any Other Excuses You Can
     Come Up With!) 61

Should I Take Social Security at 62? 75

Can I Really Live to 100? 87

Where Do I Fit Retirement Planning into My
     Jam-Packed Days? I'm Already Too Busy. 93

Parting Words 99

Resources 101

Endnotes 103

Acknowledgements 105

Meet Marcia Mantell 107

Introduction

I've had amazing opportunities to travel across America for the past 10-plus years and speak to thousands of Baby Boomer women (and men) about getting ready for retirement. The events I've attended were packed with working women in every kind of job and pay grade, including those who were at-home moms or left jobs to care for elderly family members. The women I've met were kind, caring and accomplished. And they were more than ready to stop working. Yet most of these women shared that they were scared to lose their paycheck and enter retirement.

Getting ready to retire is a big deal. The reality is that it's time to *stop worrying* about retirement and *start planning* for it. There's nothing you can change about the past, so stand up tall, take a deep breath, and dive into your future.

The more you understand the facts of your situation, the better off you will be. You have to be the one to chart your own course and know you can pay for it. Retirement should be a wonderful time in your life. You just need to get your arms around the financial realities and start building up your financial confidence. Admittedly—I'll warn you now—it will take some time and energy, longer than a weekend, but less than a decade! But, it will be well worth your efforts.

In fact, the women who tell me that they are really ready to retire all have one thing in common: they have been planning and plotting, scrimping and saving for their retirement *for years*. This is the secret to your retirement, too. Even if you feel you're getting a late start, just focus your efforts on the future. And this book is a great place to start.

Read through the chapters and you'll find that there are lots of "how to's" and resources included to help you set up your budget, make good financial decisions and learn what it takes to get to your dream retirement.

You can do it!

CHAPTER ONE

Is "Retirement" Just About the Money?

No! You can define retirement however you want ... but you'll need to pay for it.

More than a decade ago, a large financial services company aired an ad that so perfectly captured the sense of accomplishment and celebration that most of us would like to feel when we reach the finish line of our careers that I still remember it vividly today: "*Reaching Retirement is No Small Achievement.*"

That message struck a chord with me because it offered both a sense of hope that anyone could get there and a reminder that the journey to retirement is a marathon, not a sprint. Instead of running 26 miles in a few hours, it takes us 26 years to reach middle age, then another 26 years (give or take) to reach our next mile marker—the start of retirement. If we're lucky, we'll have another 26 years (or more) to make the most of living in retirement. Defining what we want to do in our retirement and being financially ready to pay for it all can be a challenge. But, just like any marathoner will tell you, the key is in the preparation, the training and mental toughness that keeps you focused on the finish line.

Discover and Celebrate Your Version of Retirement

There is a lot of discussion these days about retiring the word "retirement." Call it whatever you'd like. It's how you define those post-age 60 years that really matters. Finding meaning and joy as you enter a new uncharted chapter where you get to start every day in a new way is exciting to think about. The time you'll spend in retirement is yours and you are in control. So get ready to explore. Discover. Reinvent. Redesign. Recharge. Reimagine. Rethink. You are limited only by your imagination… and perhaps your finances.

Just as retirement is about rediscovering yourself, it's also about redefining and embracing new roles and relationships. It's a time to look back on the career you've had and the family you've created and nurtured. It's a time to bring together extended family, reconnect with friends and enjoy the role of grandma. It should be a carefree time with fewer obligations, when you can sit back and sip wine with the sisters and girlfriends who stuck with you through it all.

Reaching retirement can also be bittersweet as you acknowledge that it's time to turn some of the reins over to the younger generation. You might even shed a few tears.

In short, retirement can be your best chapter. It is a wish granted for more time to do what you want. It's your era of more freedom, fun and fulfillment. The best news of all: retirement can be anything you want it to be.

Women Control the Money—
It's Time to Take Charge

That said, retirement also has to be about the money. Doing all you want and enjoying your retirement years comes with a price tag. You want to know that you'll have enough money to make your retirement the one you want.

Unfortunately, even as we've been running the household budget and managing monthly bills and cash flow for decades, investing and high finance have not been skills that most of us have acquired over the years. That makes us uncertain and anxious about retirement finances. Don't panic here! Getting set for retirement just requires adding a more sophisticated layer of financial management to your budgeting bag of tricks. With proper planning and confidence to face your financial realities, you can do it. And frankly, you'll have to do it.

At the same time, you'll need to be aware of some hard facts that could change your financial situation over time—before or after you retire. For example,

- About 90% of women will be solely responsible for managing finances on their own at some point in their lives. (Today in the U.S., women control a total of $5 trillion to $12 trillion in total wealth, depending on the studies you read.)

- Many women will face divorce or widowhood at some point during (or even before) retirement. This can be a highly emotional period, often made worse by financial uncertainties and hardships, adjusting to and budgeting on a lower income, and cutting discretionary income.[1]

- Because women generally live longer than men, you need to be very sure that you'll have plenty of income when you're 90 or 95 or 100 years old.

So, let's get serious about retirement finances and talk about "what's the deal with retirement planning for women." There's no better time than today to get a running start on your retirement plan or to review the plans you've already made to make sure they will really work for you. You're ready to take charge of your retirement. You simply cannot afford to wait another day.

What are your dreams for retirement?

I often start retirement presentations with that very question. There are so many wonderful ideas. Two retirement goals seem to be on every Baby Boomer's list: travel and volunteering. But, when they aren't traveling, how will they fill their days? One woman planned to open a Pilates studio. A few others have mentioned moving to and working a hobby farm (one was specific about starting an organic farm). Others have waited for years to become a grandmother and they relish that role. They are happy to be the "gra-nanny" and are planning to provide full- or part-time day care for their grandchildren.

A particular favorite story is from a group of women who met in the first grade. They've stayed close friends in their hometown for the past 72 years, and are still going strong. They talk on the phone daily, have lunch together every week, and have taken a couple of road trips each year since they've been retired. They have great stories to tell and a shared past of their families. They have been there for one another through all of life's ups and downs. These "Forget-Me-Nots" represent so much that is fun and wonderful in retirement and serve as a reminder that sometimes retirement is about simplicity. It's about your best friends, your family and the enjoyment of every day.

Read how other Boomers are redefining and reinventing retirement on my blog: http://boomerretirementbriefs. com/ and post your ideas and comments.

CHAPTER TWO

How Much Will I Need for Retirement?

A million? A billion? A gazillion?
It's all about how much you will spend in retirement.

It is surprising how early it starts—a girl's discomfort with money. What to do with money, how to think about it, and how to use it wisely.

The local Rotary Club in my community sponsors a "Reality Fair" each year in May for the soon-to-be graduating seniors. They set up booths in the high school Media Center (formerly "library") and invite local merchants to participate. Among them: a realty company that shows the students how find apartments for rent; a cell phone company to talk about the cost of plan options; an insurance agent who explains renter's insurance and costs; a local bank demonstrates how to open a checking account and fill out a credit card application, discussing how interest rates work; a furniture store featuring a special deal on bedroom sets. There is also a "wheel of chance". Students spin the wheel and land on a random life situation out of their control: "you just received a $10,000 inheritance from your great uncle;" "your car was totaled in an accident;" "you violated the law and are being arrested." The town's policemen come and are a big hit when they handcuff some of the kids. The concept is great and the event is well attended by the senior class.

Prior to the event, each student fills out a brief survey, indicating a possible career. That career maps to a salary, a savings account and a student loan amount using an online database that the Rotary Club created. Every student's information was pre-loaded onto computers so each time they made a purchase at the Reality Fair, it was recorded in the database and subtracted from his or her salary or savings. A few parent volunteers run the Help Desk. As the students start on their imaginary life's journey, they buy lots of items—TVs, cell phones, cars, furniture. If they overspend their budget and savings, they could come to the Help Desk for budget counseling, advice, and guidance.

Interestingly, lots of boys came to the Help Desk fre-quently. After just a couple of purchases, they wanted to know how they were doing relative to their budget. They asked questions about how they could get a better price on various items. They wanted to know exactly how much they had left over at the end of each month. They were very interested in the interplay of their purchases against their budgets and sav-ings account balances. They asked for explanations on loan repayments and interest rates and wanted to make sure they understood why they were buying intangible items like renter's insurance. They were very engaged in the game and quick to announce that they "beat their budget" or that they "can buy a better car." They were collegial but competitive. Once one of the boys found a better deal or negotiated a lower price for something, other boys would rush over to that booth trying to get the same or a better deal.

In marked comparison, very few of the girls came to the Help Desk. When they did, they generally said that someone sent them over for help. They would ask one or two questions rather timidly, get an answer and then go back to the vendors. They did not engage the parents in any financial discussion other than the single dilemma they were dealing with. They were more often disinterested in the financial side of the game. They didn't mind the shopping around part, and tended to travel from booth to booth in groups. There was little competitive spirit or interest in financial concepts. To be fair, several of the girls were very in tune with the fact that they were getting a car from their parents, or that they knew they were going to be living at home after college so they didn't need to allocate any of their budget to rent. However, they were few and far between.

It was shocking to see such a stark contrast between boys and girls. In a high school where some 98% of the students go on to a 4-year college or university, how could there be such a wide difference between the genders when it comes to money? Why are these incredibly bright, college-bound girls not "getting it" when it comes to basic finances? How can they not be interested in the mechanics of a budget and how credit works? How will they be prepared to make important decisions for themselves that will influence the amount of money they will have as an adult? How can the girls be so unaware of the connection between career choice and salary?

It's No Surprise that Women Feel Unprepared for Retirement Finances

If our high school girls are largely disinterested and disengaged in money basics, how can we ever expect them to move ahead and find a way to fit finances, investments, fiscal policy and economics into their adult lives? This dilemma plagues women from their earliest years and comes home to roost when reaching retirement.

It's no wonder you may feel ill prepared to handle your retirement finances once that last paycheck is spent. If asked, "How much money do you need for retirement?" can you honestly and confidently answer that question? On the surface, it seems to be a simple question, yet the answer is anything but simple. To get to the real answer you'll have to ask yourself a more important question: "How much will I be spending each year in retirement?"

The banking and financial industry (traditional banks, mutual fund companies, brokerage houses, retirement plan sponsors, insurance companies, financial advisors, and so on) has struggled to find simple ways to answer these questions for years. Economists, behavioral psychologists, and professors of finance have spent decades researching them too, only to acknowledge that there is no simple answer. There is no single financial product that ensures you will have enough money for retirement or that your money will even last through retirement. The key is in the planning. There is no shortcut here. We owe it to ourselves and our families to get the facts about retirement investing and management. There are proven processes that we can follow, then tweak and adjust them to our liking. But the simple truth is the only way to ensure your successful retirement is to get more involved with your personal finances in a meaningful way.

The Numbers Tell the Story

There's a reason why there is simply no time to delay. The statistics are shocking. More than 25% of workers who are 50 or older have not saved anything at all for retirement.[2] The average retirement plan balance is only $58,000. Women have saved, on average, less than half of what men have saved and hold only about $35,000 in retirement assets.[3] So the odds are very high that you may be among those who haven't saved enough. Even if you have managed to amass $500,000 to $1 million or more for retirement, that may not be enough to meet all of your retirement needs and wishes.

There is a general guideline for tapping your retirement savings for income in retirement: Plan to take out only about 4% of your savings in the first year if you retire at age 65. If you retire earlier, take less. That means, if you'll need $20,000 a year from your savings starting at age 65, your nest egg needs to have about $500,000 in it. It also means that taking out 10% is much too high. You'll likely deplete your retirement money in just a handful of years.

An important step in figuring out your numbers is to create a comprehensive retirement income plan online or on paper. You'll find a budget worksheet planner in Chapter 5 that is a good place to start. Or, find an online retirement income planning tool that, after some data entry, will illustrate how much you may need for income in retirement. Try the Retirement Income Planner (and other retirement planning tools) at www.Fidelity.com or the Retirement Income

Calculator at www.TRowePrice.com. If you are working with a financial advisor, ask him or her to run a specific retirement income plan for you.

Then when you're asked "How much money do you need for retirement?" you'll be able to answer that question with a high degree of confidence. Practice saying: "I need as much money as I am going to spend. And, I'm going to take the time I need to plan and figure out just how much money that is."

That's a much better answer than guessing that you need a "gazillion" dollars!

"You can find everything on Amazon!"

Every year we live in retirement will be another year of spending. I often share with my audiences that I plan to live a long life and will be shopping until the end. Here's the advice I received from one 90 year old woman:

When asked how she spent her days, she said they were full and interesting. She enjoys lunches with her friends and reading. She likes how easy it is to stay connected—using email to keep up with her extended family. She also likes how easy it is these days to shop. No need to walk into town to buy something at a store. No more driving to the mall and fighting for a parking spot. Now, she has the whole world of choices right at her fingertips. "After all," she said, "you can find everything on Amazon!"

That gave me great insight into the fact that not only will we be shopping in our old age, but with technology, it will be so much easier. Think about who you buy for today and where you spend your shopping dollars. Now, assume you'll do the same all the way through your retirement. What will be on your list and how much might those items cost in 20, 30 or 40 years into the future?

CHAPTER THREE

Why is Retirement Different for Women?

Because we've spent our adult lives as the family CEO, not the CFO; the President of our household, not the Chief Investment Officer (CIO).

If you look at how successful companies are run, each person in the senior ranks has a specific area of expertise that he or she brings to the organization. No one person or department does everything; rather, each offers up his or her skills to meet the overall company's goals. The Chief Executive Officer (CEO) or President defines its mission. Without the CEO there are no clear directions, no specific goals, and no one holding everyone else accountable. The Chief Financial Officer (CFO) and CIO are critical for the financial survival of the firm.

In a smaller way, our own households run like mini corporations. Whether it's just you, or you plus a spouse or partner, or you, a spouse/partner and a gaggle of kids, there's usually some division of labor, often based on areas of expertise. If you live alone, you have prioritized the functions that you can do personally, have found good resources to support you, and may have farmed out certain tasks to experts where you pay for their services.

If you look at the structure of your home as a chief executive might think about the departments in a company, there are many areas of expertise needed to run it efficiently. Here is a comparison of a few typical functions and tasks:

Function in a Corporation	Tasks in a Household
Accounting	Paying bills, budgeting, and cash management
Human Resources	Raising children to adulthood and letting them go
Employee Benefits	Meal prep, grocery shopping, menu planning and clean-up, laundry, cleaning, helping with homework, transportation, health care
Strategic Planning	Organizing daily life, running the family calendar, figuring out how to be in 4 places at the same time, planning sleepovers, date nights and vacations
Market Research	PTA, sports or music events, religious communities, neighbors, community service
Sales and Marketing	Clipping coupons, buying on sale, supporting certain vendors, creating relationships with stores and service providers
Communications	Dinner table, texting, family game night, notes in lunchboxes, negotiating a reasonable curfew
Information Technology	Deciphering cell phone plans, buying electronics, computer upgrades and security, monitoring activities, identity theft protection
Board of Directors	You, Spouse or Partner, outside advisors
Finance	Investing for retirement, college, long-term and short-term goals, house maintenance, tax planning

Women Just Get Things Done

In a corporation with many employees, the CEO is steering the ship, setting the goals, and is responsible for an overall smooth operation. At home, someone also functions as the CEO, and typically, that is the woman. Women have a tremendous capacity to run their own personal empires—from hundreds of daily to-do's, to raising kids, to getting dinner on the table, and everything in between. In addition to being CEO, women often take on the role of budget planner, bill payer, cash flow manager, and saver. Like the "accounting" department of a company, women deal with the day-to-day expenses of the household and often focus on making sure every dollar is stretched as far as possible.

To be clear, this ability to manage household finances is a tremendous skill and one that you may not even realize you have. The attention to detail it requires and the need to juggle multiple money priorities at once is critical to keeping the household afloat. It shouldn't be tossed aside as "a routine part of my day" or "just something I do". This is a real job in the corporate world. Employees in the accounting department get paid very well to make sure bills are paid on time, to keep ample cash in the bank to meet payroll, and to negotiate for better pricing. It's just that at home we don't get paid for our accounting skills. We just get it done.

Investing is Not Accounting

But there is another financial skill that women are often not as familiar and comfortable with: investing. This is a completely different area that has very little to do with accounting. Investing is the art and science of making your money grow based on a careful assessment of your ability to handle risk in the financial markets. Said more simply, it's your comfort with losing money in a falling market.

Investing is a fascinating, complex area, handled in companies by the CFO or Chief Investment Officer and staff. It is a discipline that encompasses economic principals, monetary policy, and financial market activities. It requires an in-depth understanding of how the company and its earnings are affected by global economic forces like market fluctuations, access to capital, currency valuations, inflation, and real estate trends. There are sophisticated mathematical algorithms involved to select and manage investment portfolios that can grow or preserve corporate dollars without taking on too much risk. Those who love these kinds of topics spend their days immersed in the language and activities of the financial markets. Thank goodness we have those people because not all of us want to spend our days reading the latest earnings reports or checking on international monetary policies!

Of course, if we only had a crystal ball, all of us—including the corporate CIO—could clearly see when the next recession is coming and when to buy and sell investments so that we never lose any of our money. Well, that is simply not going to happen. That's why every household, as well as every company, needs both a good "accountant" and a good "finance" person. So ask yourself: are you the accountant keeping track of all the cash or are you the financial investor balancing risks with rewards to grow your money for longer term goals? (It's great if you answered that you are both. You're ahead of the curve.)

Women Have the Skills, but Lack Time—and Confidence

Interestingly, women have the skills to be wise investors. They are relatively risk-adverse, cautious and deliberate in choosing investments, and thoughtful in decision making, taking more time when deciding to buy or sell. In fact, a number of academic studies over the past fifteen years have shown that women tend to be better investors than men, doing more of the right things to make good decisions to grow their money. One study found that men trade 45% more than women. The net result is that the guys saw a reduction of their net returns by some 2.65%, while the reduction in net returns for the ladies was only 1.72%.[4] That is a significant difference. During the severe market downturn in 2008-2009, men were more likely to sell at market lows than women, locking in greater losses.[5]

For women, the issue around investing often may be less about skills and more about a lack of time. Busy women just don't have the time in their hectic days to become savvy investors. Even women who have retirement savings plans at work often don't think of themselves as "investors." They know it takes specific skills to build a portfolio for retirement, to understand the balance between risk and reward, and to stay calm when the economy moves into a recession. (On average, the US experiences a recessionary period every five to six years. That's a lot of market downturns over a lifetime!)

There's also that question of confidence in entering what has traditionally been a male-dominated world. For generations, the stock market, futures markets and financial investing was a virtual men's club and today the investment industry is still dominated by men. So it's no surprise that the approach, the language, and the information are presented in ways that work best for men.

Fortunately, the Internet is a great equalizer. You can now take full advantage of all the information out there to increase your knowledge about investing for your retirement and get ready access to the tools you need to make wise investment decisions. It gives you a way to learn the language and play the game.

They're Asking the Wrong Question about Women and Investing

Many people in the finance and investment world have wrestled with the question, "Why aren't women more confident investors?" That's probably not the right question. Instead, we might turn it around and ask: "Why *would* women be confident investors?" What has prepared a woman to know about economic and monetary policy, risk and volatility measures, and the behavior of the stock and bond markets? What education and training in a girl's upbringing or a woman's experience running her household sets her up to become a successful and savvy investor? Recognizing that women look at risk, assess losses, and just think differently goes a long way toward understanding why we are a different breed of investors—any why we need to approach retirement investing in a way that works for us.

It's helpful to realize that women may have a different orientation toward investing because we have been raised to do different things. Our focus, regardless of how big and successful our outside careers have become, is still on nurturing our families and managing day-to-day living expenses. We want to ensure our households run as smoothly as possible to make ends meet while raising our children to be independent, successful adults. We connect with our communities and hold our extended families together.

After meeting hundreds of daily obligations, there is simply nothing left at the end of the day to learn to be a more confident investor. It is no surprise then that the role of household CFO or CIO is very often delegated either to the male or is delegated to professional financial advisors.

Put Yourself First, For a Change

Women concentrate their time and efforts on doing special things for those who are important to us. Consequently, our own needs fall to the sideline. But as we begin to focus more on our retirement, we need to start putting ourselves first. That means:

- Thinking of retirement planning as a merger between two different and unique business disciplines, where you become both the CEO and CFO and integrate cash flow management with retirement investing and finances.

- Becoming a more confident investor by embracing your skills and expanding your financial "knowledge bank." This includes learning about Social Security and Medicare well before reaching retirement.

- Carving out time to learn the ropes about investing, using the online the resources available to every in- vestor today—or the assistance of a trusted, qualified financial advisor.

As women, we might not have had the opportunity to grow up thinking of ourselves as investors or finding time to learn about investing as we reared our children and built our careers, but that doesn't mean we can't jump in now. We're not finished learning and are certainly capable of becoming confident investors. Retirement is too important to leave to chance, hope, and a winning lottery ticket.

Use your shoe shopping skills to save more for retirement:

For every pair of shoes you buy, put the same amount of money into an Individual Retirement Account (IRA) that's in your name. Make sure your savings is going into an appropriate investment (stock or mutual fund) that you have researched. This simple technique can help you build your own personal savings for retirement. The IRA is in your name, giving you control and independence over some of your retirement assets.

For more information on IRAs, read Chapter 4.

CHAPTER FOUR

How Big Is Your "Freedom Fund"?

It should be big enough to make a difference to you or someone you choose.

Many women of the Boomer generation have been part of a couple for 30 or more years by now. They may have worked outside the home or have been at-home moms. They may have built a successful career or juggled raising children and working part-time. They soared to great heights and put Band-Aids on little fingers. While managing the day-to-day lives and activities of their families, too many have missed out on building some key financial skills that single women have known about for years. Very often, married women haven't built an adequate credit history, amassed a sufficient balance in their IRAs, or set aside a substantial cash reserve in their own name. It's time to change all that!

Don't Forget that You are an Individual, Too

Married women need to think about themselves as individuals, not just as the better half of a couple. The retirement and financial worlds generally operate and recognize individuals based on each Social Security number. Think about how you are set up as an individual in the eyes of a financial firm or credit agency. Do you know what your financial profile looks like from an outsider's view? It matters. Women who have been single for a long time are often way ahead of married women in terms of establishing their financial freedom. They are their own financial decision makers and have found ways to ensure that their credit history is in good shape. If you are married, take a page from the single ladies' book and make sure you will be ready when you find yourself living on our own.

There are many reasons why married women often assign or abdicate various financial aspects of their lives to their men. It might be because some men seem more confident and capable with financial topics. (They might not be, but they can sure sound like they know what they are talking about!) It might be that once children arrive, a mother simply does not have the time or energy to take on investing strategies in addition to the two thousand new jobs that just fell on her shoulders. It could be that finances are just not talked about in her social circles, so she doesn't benefit from other points of view. We're always happy to talk about our children, the latest Hollywood gossip, and what's going on in the neighborhood, but for some reason, money and finances do not make it to the list of lunch topics. We talk openly about many "M" topics: our marriages and our mothers, mammograms and meno-pause misery, a good merlot and the best martinis. Rarely, if ever, do we talk about money.

Why married women are often less comfortable with money matters is not really the point. We just need to recog-nize that the integration of our lives with our men has resulted, more often than not, into a "joint arrangement" where all money is "our" money. That's not a bad thing for running the household budget, but unfortunately, it can be a problem for building a woman's financial profile and record. The bottom line is that in many joint financial arrangements, only one person is building an adequate credit history in the eyes of the financial world. In this day and age having a solid credit history is essential. It helps provide you with the financial freedom you need to secure the best credit, the lowest interest rates and the protection you'll need if you find yourself on your own. It takes years to build a good credit history.

Credit history is built on a few key factors:

- Demonstrating that you can manage debt over long periods of time. This means you need to have debt (revolving debt such as credit cards as well as install-ment loan debt such as auto loans or school loans), pay it on time and not over-extend your limits.

- Demonstrating that you can manage timely payments of recurring bills over long periods of time. Utility bills, technology bills and the like that show ownership and a payment history.

Individual Ownership

There are specific limitations to "joint accounts" in financial services and credit agencies. Depending on exactly how that joint account is structured it may really mean "his account." If you and your spouse have "joint" credit cards then both of you are equally on the hook for paying the full amount of outstand-ing debt. You both build credit history from this arrangement—and it can be either good or bad. If, however, you are only listed as an "authorized user" on the credit card, you can use it for purchases, but only he is building a credit history.

Look at your cell phone bill. Whose name is on it? How about your cable bill? There is only one name listed and typically, it will be your husband's (unless you happened to open the original contract in your name). There is no "joint ownership" for cell phones and cable providers because they can only attach one Social Security number to each contract. Even when she is paying the bills, the credit history is being built in his name, putting her at a disadvantage. (That also means that only his credit history is docked if there is a delinquency.)

It is critical to understand the facts and realities about building your own credit history. Take the necessary steps to ensure you are creating your own financial profile and credit history. It's not too late to make changes to establish yourself in the eyes of the financial world. Generally, you'll find the steps quite simple:

- If you do not have a credit card in just your name, it's time to get one. Call the bank or credit union where you have your checking account and talk to them about applying for a credit card. Establish credit at your favorite place to shop—a department store, Target, or Home Goods, etc. Most large stores issue credit cards and you should have one or two in your name (plus, you often get better deals when using a store card for your purchases). You'll want to limit your spending on these cards to no more than 50% of the credit line and never miss a payment. Demonstrate excellent management of your credit to build a strong credit history and credit score.

- Take a look at your monthly household bills—from electric, gas, water, cable TV, and cell phones to maintenance contracts. See if any are in your name (or show your name first.) If not, call one or two of the services and ask how you can transfer the bill into your name. Credit bureaus check with utility companies for late payments or delinquencies. Only the individual whose name is on the account gets credit for reliable and timely payment habits. You can increase your credit-worthiness after one or two of your household bills are transferred to your name. Just remember to put them on "auto-pay" so that payments always arrive on time.

- Do you own your own car? Often, our husbands shop for new cars. The car is officially in his name as is the auto loan. Next time you are in the market for a new car, make sure you are listed as the owner and that you take the loan out in your name. Then, pay the loan on time every month.

Building your good credit is a must-do:

Getting a good handle on your credit score is critical. Your credit score determines many financial opportunities, such as qualifying for a mortgage and at what interest rate; the credit line amount a store will grant you on a credit card; if you can get a cell phone contract on your own; and, if you can secure a car loan in your own name. In fact, it's very hard to even get a credit card in your name if you don't have a credit score.

There is great information online about what goes into your credit score, how credit cards work, and how you can influence your credit score. Take a look at the Khan Academy (www.KhanAcademy.org) under the economics and finance section for several excellent videos that explain how credit cards work. You might also take a look at the Khan Academy videos on the Bank of America website. There is an excellent video on how your FICO score is determined and how your credit score is calculated. (If you don't know what FICO stands for, you really need to watch these videos!) Just go to www.bettermoneyhabits.com. The information is invaluable.

Managing Your Debt

Debt is a huge issue for women (and families). The older and the closer to retirement we get, the more challenging debt management can be. Servicing debt for items you bought last year or two years ago can be crippling when you need to redirect more money to save for retirement. The level of debt among older Americans has been increasing significantly. More than half of Americans over age 65 carry a significant amount of debt: Twenty-nine percent still carry a mortgage while 18% have debt from home equity credit lines or loans against their retirement plans. Twenty-seven percent have credit card debt and 16% are still paying down car or truck loans.[6] Squarely addressing the debt situation in your household should happen well before retirement. You cannot ignore the financial realities of accumulated debt and the impact it will have on your retirement. Modifying any behavior can be very difficult (think of all those diets you've tried) and changing decades of spending habits will not happen overnight, but getting ready to retire so that you will be as comfortable as possible is critically important. These steps should help you get a start on reducing your debt:

- Understand your full debt picture—Make a list of all your outstanding debts including mortgage, auto, and school loans, retirement plan loans (401(k), 403(b), etc.) and add up all of those credit card balances.

- Determine what "good debt" is—usually your mortgage interest and perhaps a HELOC (home equity line of credit) since you can take a tax deduction for this debt.

- Quickly pay down debts with exorbitant interest rates—usually credit cards.

Until you are properly managing your debt rather than debt managing you, you are compromising your retirement future.

Make Sure You Are Credit-Worthy

As a woman of the 21st century, you need to be financially confident and independent. You'll want to know that the crediting agencies see you as credit-worthy. Prepare now so that you'll be able to manage your own assets during retirement. This is not to say that you and your husband should change how you are running everything in your household. It is to say that in today's world each individual person is considered for loans, credit, and financial advantages based on his or her personal financial record. If you don't have a financial record based on your Social Security number, there is nothing to go on. There is no such thing as a "joint" record.

In addition to building a strong credit history, women should have independent control over at least two buckets of money that are exclusively hers: an IRA and a "freedom fund". These should be separate from the household money and savings, and should not be an emergency fund. These are investment accounts that are owned by and managed by her. In fact, her husband or partner should have separate but equal accounts as well.

Your IRA

The first account every woman should have is an IRA—an Individual Retirement Account—for her future retirement. Notice that the "I" in IRA stands for "individual." Interestingly, when it comes to retirement, the laws are written for each person individually. There are no such things as joint IRAs, joint retirement accounts, or even joint Social Security or Medicare. IRAs are powerful financial products. They are essentially "lock boxes" of retirement assets. They are savings that you put aside specifically for your spending in retirement.

There are significant tax advantages to IRAs, but most importantly, only you can decide when to take the money out and to whom you want to pass the assets when you die. No one can influence your beneficiary decision because it is strictly up to you to name the beneficiary. This is unlike a workplace plan such as a 401(k) or 403(b). With a workplace plan, married workers are generally required to name their spouse as the sole beneficiary unless he signs a document giving up his rights to inherit this money. Everyone can have an IRA so long as you have wages and generally are younger than 70. This means that either you worked and earned a paycheck, or if married and filing taxes jointly, your spouse has wages for the year. An IRA is an excellent account for building some financial independence for retirement.

Your Freedom Fund

The second account that every woman should have is a "free-dom fund". This is simply an individual savings or investment account at a financial institution or bank—not a joint account or a savings account that is attached to your joint checking ac-count. It gets funded over time with amounts your household finances allow. It will be invested by you, the decisions will be yours, and there is no approval or veto power by your spouse. If you want a girls' weekend in Vegas, terrific. If you want a special piece of jewelry, go buy it. Your spouse/partner should also have the same type of account in his name. Be ready if he goes out and buys a motorcycle with his freedom fund!

The freedom funds are separate accounts from the household checkbook so that each of you has some financial wiggle room to do some of the things that you want on your terms. You also control who inherits these assets. You'll need to make sure you set up a "TOD" on the account—a transfer on death order. This is different than a beneficiary form, but equally important to do. That the account is only in your name also helps build more financial independence, an added bonus. Once you set up your freedom fund, you're ready to start directing some of your household assets into it.

Building the MFF:

My husband came up with the concept of the freedom fund and named mine the "Marcia Freedom Fund". Some years ago I worked at a job where I received a bonus. We were quite young and managing our finances to make ends meet. The bonus money was like found treasure.

He suggested how we could spend the money: a new lawn sprinkler system, paying for daycare, reducing credit card debt, a vacation. True, these were all needs that we had, but spending "free" money on needs didn't feel quite right. I knew I wanted to eventually quit my job and take a year off to stay home with our girls, but we could not afford to lose my paycheck. If we banked the bonus money, it could eventually replace my paycheck for that year at home. It was a hard decision to save this windfall when we needed and wanted so many other things. My husband agreed that the money could be "mine" and I should set up a separate account that I owned. We would save my bonus money to build up my freedom fund, the MFF.

It turned out that I didn't get to leave my job for several more years. When I did, I started my own company and didn't need to tap the MFF after all. So, I will continue to keep my money for something else…maybe for our daughters' weddings someday…

You'll find a checklist at boomerretirementbriefs.com for some suggestions on building your own personal financial profile.

CHAPTER FIVE

Why Is Shoe Shopping Important for Your Retirement?

It's just the start of a woman's "designer budget plan."

If there is anything that women around the world are known for, it's our shoes. It's fascinating to see the closets of the rich and famous filled with shoes of every color and style. Most of us Boomers remember the global media drama that unfolded around Imelda Marcos, the wife of the former Philippines leader. When he was overthrown and the palace was opened to the poor masses, they found more than 3,000 pairs of her shoes. Our reputation for buying shoes is legendary. We know shoes really can make the outfit, and we envy those women who can put together a smashing outfit with just the right shoes every time.

One study calculated the average amount of money women spend on their shoes over a lifetime. We buy somewhere around 268 pairs of shoes between the ages 18—60 and spend an average of $20,000![7]

Continuing to Shop in Retirement

When you really think about it, is there any reason that you won't be shopping once you reach retirement? No. When you have a lot more time on your hands, won't you likely be doing more and going more places? The need for shoe shopping (among other things) could actually increase.

Just because we will be retired does not mean that our general daily lifestyle will radically change. Certain things will change, of course. We won't be racing out of the house to get to work on time. We won't have to fit all of our errands into the weekend. We can make dinner at a reasonable hour. From a day-to-day and a week-to-week view, our habits and preferences usually continue in retirement. We'll shop for birthday gifts and plan parties for our family and friends. We'll make the get-together's special, buying new toys and crafts for the grandchildren and paying for various activities. We'll host more dinners and splurge at a few favorite restaurants. We might take on a more active role supporting our aging parents or in-laws, aunts, and uncles, and elderly friends which could include financial support. Many of us will take on the role of family matriarch around the same time we're ready to retire. As matriarch, we'll host more events and spend more money to bring the family together and keep up family traditions. So much of our day involves shopping for others and supporting our families that we don't even realize how much it all adds up.

Preparing for the reality of how you will shop throughout your retirement is a must-do. It is not always easy to think of all the ways you'll spend your money or put a price tag on some of the items you'll purchase. Traditional budget work-sheets from financial companies don't work well for women.

They are too focused on maintenance items and taxes and broad financial categories. While those are very important and must be included, there is simply no room to estimate costs where women spend money.

Retirement budgets are most effective when you can organize your spending into essential items (those that you must have) and discretionary spending (the nice-to-haves). How you define your "essential" items will become the basis for figuring out your retirement income needs. Since discretionary expenses, by definition, need to be flexible and may not occur in certain years or economic conditions, you'll want to first focus on building a specific plan that ensures that your essential expenses are fully covered every year in retirement. What exactly will you consider to be your essential budget items?

Too often women's "shopping" or "spending" is overlooked, dismissed or not even considered when building a traditional retirement income plan. We don't fit neatly into a standardized form that a financial advisor might typically use. Money for another new pair of shoes or for something for the family is an essential expense. Providing for our loved ones in ways both big and small is what we do. We care for our families and friends and keep the connections we've built over 30, 40, 50 plus years. That's what we do best and that does not change when we enter retirement. The dollars to support these purchases just need to be factored into our retirement budgets.

Spending on the grandchildren is an essential expense:

Is there anything more wonderful than becoming a grandparent? Finally, your reward for all those years you spent raising your children and all the sacrifices you made along the way. But now you have your legacy, your blessing. It is no wonder grandparents might indulge those grandchildren from time to time.

One grandfather remarked that his wife was "spending a fortune" on clothes and toys for their new grandchildren. She just laughed and said that she hadn't yet filled the entire closet in the guest room with new things for the babies. In fact, she was heading back to the mall. Who would say no to a grandmother who is buying for her grandchildren!

Where is this kind of essential expense listed in traditional retirement budgets?

Build Your Retirement Budget Planner for How You Really Spend Money

Women run their household budgets well. They will run their retirement household budgets just as well. It will be helpful to see where your money is going to be spent in retirement, how much various items might cost, and where you'll get the money to pay for these items. Using a budget planner designed from a woman's point of view will help fit your family's needs into your retirement and figure out how you'll pay for them. These four steps are a good starting point (see the chart that follows for more details).

1. Create your list of personal essential expenses—from buying for the grandchildren to flying family members home for the holidays. Include your shopping, hobbies that will fill your days, and support for family members as needed.

2. Capture special events that you will plan and host for family and friends such as holidays and weddings that will occur in the coming years.

3. Fill in the typical "essential" expenses that any good financial planner would recommend: food, shelter, health care, basic transportation, taxes, and the like.

4. Identify items that are truly discretionary. These are expenses that can be delayed or eliminated in years when the market is taking a downturn.

Once your list is complete, it's time to put a price tag on each item. A rough estimate or a guess is good enough to get started. You can always refine the information later. The point is that your retirement budget planner should show you and your spouse/partner where your money will be spent in retirement. Don't skimp on the planner. Think of as much as you can and get it on paper.

Running Out of Money in Retirement— A Scary Thought

Most surveys taken over the past decade find that about half of all Americans are concerned about running out of money in retirement, and women tend to be even more worried about the prospect of outliving their savings. Even many higher earning families are concerned that they won't have enough to maintain their lifestyle. After all, if you are spending say

$100,000 a year and aren't planning drastic cuts in spending once you reach retirement, you'll still need to generate $100,000 each year once that paycheck stops. Will you have a large enough nest egg to draw from to support your lifestyle? Better to know well before you enter retirement than to be shocked after you leave your job.

Approach budget planning in a very personal way. Make your lists and estimate how much the various categories might cost. This planner should help you understand how your retirement spending needs to be managed and helps you communicate where your money needs to be allocated. This budget planner has been designed for women to own their retirement expenses while continuing to do what they do best—keeping the family together through the years and across the generations.

You can download a free copy of the expanded budget planner at BoomerRetirementBriefs.com

Planning for Retirement—from a Woman's Perspective

1—Personal Essential Items & Activities: Staying Connected with Family and Friends

Items and activities that are central to how women nurture and cultivate their important communities and connections are essential expenses. They are non-negotiable, but spending can increase/decrease based on overall financial picture and frequency:

- Keeping the family together activities
- Spending time with friends activities
- Recognizing special days and events
- Outings with family and friends
- Bringing the kids/grandkids home
- Grandkids

- Supporting church, charity, community
- Gifts for family and close friends
- Hobbies, crafts, gardening, photography, etc.
- Support for aging parents, relatives, special needs adult children
- Add your own…

2—Essential Special Events for Friends and Family

Making sure that important people get together periodically is especially important when they are scattered around the globe. Women typically plan holiday gatherings, weddings, and reunions, and need to plan for the price tag as well as the party:

- Plane tickets—for you or others you are paying for
- Party food / party fare / decorations
- Holidays
- Gifts for family, friends

- Weddings—daughter(s), son(s), other family and friends
- Reunions—high school, college, family
- New outfits/accessories/shoes for special events
- Add your own…

3—Monthly Household Essential Expenses (traditional categories)

These are all the basics to keep the household running. These items must be supported every month as long as you or your spouse/partner is alive including:

• Food	• Car/maintenance/gas
• House maintenance & mortgage/rent	• Utilities
• Taxes	• Technology/computers/ staying connected
• Health care expenditures	• Other

4—Household Discretionary Expenses

The extras that you can scale back or give up in years where your savings may be lower than ideal. Items that you can trade off from time to time as needed, such as:

• Vacations	• Memberships to social clubs
• Car purchases	• Gifting assets to children
• Dining out frequently	• Gifting / college savings for grandchildren
• Optional "nice to have" home improvements	• Other
• Extensive hobbies	

CHAPTER SIX

Remember "Because I Said So!"?

Those famous words from your parents that you promised yourself you would never say to your kids can serve you well when planning for retirement.

We've all made the same promise to ourselves. By the age of 10, we just knew that we would never tell our own kids (or nieces and nephews) "Because I said so!" when they asked questions. We vowed that we would be reasonable and patiently listen to a child's point of view, not automatically saying "No!" to their outrageous requests. We remember how frustrating it was to work at a fast food restaurant or some other job when all our friends were hanging out at the pool, so we would never tell our kids to "get a job!" But then, quite surprisingly, it slips out one day when the two-year-old just won't stop asking "why," and it continues through the teen years when you're just too tired to battle over that mini skirt or curfew or tattoo or another piercing yet another time. By the time that child reaches sixteen, you are telling them to get out and get a job! "There's no free lunch and I'm tired of paying for your things when you don't even appreciate them!" We can laugh now, but it was quite a shock when we heard our parents' voices coming out of our own mouths.

In dark of night when no one is around and we're being honest, we have to admit our parents were quite right. Their words of wisdom helped us raise our kids in a fast-paced world. And now those same time-honored phrases can serve you well as you deal with the realities of getting ready to retire. You may have other favorite sayings that you remember, so feel free to add them to your list. Since most of us have not yet saved enough for the retirement we would like, these little pearls of wisdom can get us back on track and better prepared for the financial obligations retirement will bring.

Making Trade-Offs

"No" is probably the single most important word we should be using when it comes to retirement finances. We have to say no to some of the extras today to prepare for tomorrow. This is a basic trade-off. Give up something today or change some spending habits now and redirect that money into retirement savings.

It is important to save as much as possible for retirement, but how much is enough? There are any number of guidelines that have valid underlying assumptions. They vary widely, but all use a baseline that depends on how much you will spend in retirement. Which one might fit your personal situation?

- A long-held belief has been that you'll need to save enough to generate 80% to 100% of your pre-retirement income for each year of retirement, depending on your spending rate.

- One financial firm suggests that you'll need to have saved 8 times your ending salary to ensure your lifestyle can be maintained.[8]

- From some early research back in 2008, one firm showed how certain retirees may need to aim for spending at 120% over their ending salary due to the increases in health care costs.[9]

Any way you slice it, you need to replace the income you currently receive by way of your paycheck. While some retirees drastically downsize how they live once they reach retirement, most do not. You should be preparing aggressively now to pay for every year of your retirement. A common dilemma for many women is that they find it hard to say no to things for their family. Getting into strong savings habits can be challenging, but it can be done. It takes some practice and trial and error. It's often a shift in your mindset. Setting aside more money for retirement is not selfish. It's actually a gift you will give your family. It allows you to plan for a long retirement where you remain independent without burdening your loved ones (another of women's biggest fears) in old age.

Super-Save

If you haven't saved enough for your retirement, it's time to start "super saving". Every dollar you save now will pay you back two or three dollars in your old age. Make sure you pay yourself first and make it automatic. Retirement plans offered through an employer use that approach. Before you get your paycheck, your 401(k) or 403(b) contributions have been pulled aside and safely placed in your retirement account. Use that same approach for your IRA and freedom fund by setting up automatic feeds from your paycheck or your checking account every month. It only takes three easy steps to set up automated feeds into your retirement accounts:

1. Put your bank's routing number and checking account number on the IRA new account form (or attach a voided check).

2. Select "automatic" contributions.

3. Choose a monthly amount that you can redirect from your household budget directly into your IRA.

Bribes and rewards can work to make trade-offs easier:

Try rewarding yourself for good savings behavior. If you've traded your day at the spa or reduced spending on new clothes and directed those dollars to your IRA, find a non-financial way to reward yourself for those important actions. Check out your local library for free events in your local area and passes to museums and shows.

Another idea that may work to increase your savings is finding a few budget items that are flexible, such as premium cable channels or eating out, where you could scale back. Then, "bribe" yourself into better behavior! Each time you don't eat out, pay yourself $20. If your cable bill drops by $50 a month, pocket that $50. Deposit your "bribe" money each month directly into your IRA.

You'll be surprised by how your retirement savings can grow over a few years when you make small deposits each month.

Every little bit adds up over time. Let's say you can set aside $100 each month into your IRA. It could be worth about $60,000 after 25 years at a 5% real rate of return. If you can super-save $300 each month into your IRA, that could grow to about $180,000 after 25 years.[10] If you are thinking that you are too old or it's too late for any savings to really make a difference, rethink that point of view! It's never too late to become a good saver.

Keep Working, or Get Back to Work

Over the generations, women have made tremendous strides in the workforce and now comprise some 55%—60% of all US workers.[11] They virtually work in every type of job and field and can have jobs and careers that span 40 to 50 years. There is an ongoing discussion about the wage gap. It is real. It is there. On average, women are paid less for the same job as men, earning on average 78% of a man's paycheck. The gap widens as we age.[12] The consequences for women's retirement readiness can be significant when you earn less than you should right from the beginning.

Now that you're approaching retirement, you've got some decisions to make about how long to keep working. If you've built a career already, you may want to continue working at full capacity in your current job, or you may want to try your hand at something else either full-time or part-time. Either way, keeping a paycheck coming in under your own name and work history might be a more important retirement decision than you realize. It's not only about having some of your own money to control and direct, but it's also about saving the most you can for your old age and setting up your Social Security benefits for the most you could be entitled to.

There are examples everywhere of women continuing to work well into their 60s. One senior executive moved from financial services to a management position at the Red Cross. Another senior marketing manager switched from corporate marketing to teaching marketing at a local university. After 20 years as an emergency room nurse on the evening shift, one woman changed course to a less stressful nursing job during the day. In each case, their salary dropped somewhat, but there were many benefits to continuing to work full-time. Each woman

- Continued to be valued and contribute on the job;

- Expanded her network, meeting new people in new areas;

- Added more to retirement savings accounts and strengthened their work record for Social Security benefits; and,

- Delayed tapping their nest eggs as long as possible.

Your Work History Directly Impacts Your Social Security Benefits

Your actual Social Security payment will be calculated based on your personal earnings record, so you'll want as robust a record as possible. Social Security calculates your benefit based on your highest 35 years of earnings. They do not have to be consecutive years of earnings, just 35 years in total. Let's say you started working at 18 and now you are 63 and thinking about your retirement. That's 45 years of work history. Social Security will use your highest 35 years of income and run a calculation for you. Now, let's say you took 15 years out of the work force to raise your children. In this case, you only have 30 years of earnings on record and your calculation will include five years of zero dollars. You may have the option to work for another 5 years to help improve your Social Security benefit.

Every earnings record will be unique and individual based on your personal work history. You can find your full work record on your Social Security statement. It is a powerful tool.

Take the time to really look at your current statement before you make decisions about when you could stop working. Decide if you can increase your benefit by replacing some of the years where you had low earnings or no earnings. You'll find your Social Security statement at www.ssa.gov. It's easy to set up your account and login at "my Social Security" on the home page.

Retiring Too Early Can Limit Your Retirement Income

The average retirement age for women in the US is about 62.[13] Remaining on the job longer than perhaps you were originally planning can make a significant difference to your retirement as it:

- Keeps a paycheck coming in so you don't have to start drawing on your savings;

- Lets you continue super-saving into retirement accounts;

- Allows you to wait to claim Social Security, likely resulting in a larger payment later; and,

- Buys you more time to make sure you are really financially prepared to stop that paycheck.

Work also provides a strong social network and a solid structure to your day. Many women say that being around younger workers helps keep them young. If you can wait even a year or two later to retire, your financial picture should be brighter.

Try changing directions so you can take full advantage of all that working offers. Developing an "encore career" or "second act" may be a key to your retirement success. Once the kids are gone and you have more time to think about the best next career move, cast your net wide. Find something you want to do, keep that paycheck coming and think about how your ultimate retirement picture will improve. Considering what you will do next takes some exploration, some time, and often a bit of trial and error. It is never too late to find a way to collect a paycheck…you just might need to be more creative about landing that next job.

Can You Start a Career Later in Life?

What if you didn't work outside the home or stopped working to raise your family or to care for an aging relative? Can you get back into the workforce at this late date? The short answer is yes. The real answer is that it may be harder than you would like. Age discrimination is alive and well in most industries and it may take some time to land a job. Don't let that discourage you. Square those shoulders, stand with your head held high and give it a try. You aren't looking for a job that pays six-figures. You have something to offer and are more than capable of working for a paycheck. So go get it. Even if you have been out of the workforce for some time, you have a lifetime of skills and abilities. You just might be lacking some confidence when asked about what you can bring to the table. You'll get better after you have several interviews.

For any woman looking for a new job, there are a few things that can help you be more confident:

- **Get tech savvy.** If you don't have good, basic computer skills, start there. Take a class at your adult education center or at a community college and become familiar with Microsoft Office Word, Excel and PowerPoint. These tools are as critical as typing skills were 30 and 40 years ago.

- **Be social.** Be able to talk about how you use social media, from Facebook to Twitter to Pinterest, and others. Learn to use a few features and apps on a smartphone and start texting. It's fun to do and you'll feel that you are keeping up with the younger generation.

- **Check resources.** There are innovative resources out there today for the 50-plus job seeker. AARP is a good place to start. Look for local groups that help with encore careers, the next chapter and doing what's next.

- **Do your homework.** With extensive resources available online today, you'll get a feel for the company culture just by checking out their website. Sounding knowledgeable about the company shows you cared enough to do some thoughtful research.

- **Use your personal network.** The best way to land a job is through your personal network. Tell everyone you know that you are looking for a new job.

Take your time and enjoy the process of meeting new people and talking about what you can do for them. Be current, use your resources, and prepare well!

Starting Your Own Business

If working for someone else isn't your favorite idea, do your own thing. One stay-at-home mom got her real estate license after her last child started high school. That didn't turn out to be a passion. She ended up leveraging what she learned in real estate plus her love of photography to start her own real estate staging company. Very creative. We've all heard of women who started baking out of their kitchens or sewing wraps for kids at the beach. Just watch Shark Tank for inspiration if you have an idea you want to pursue.

Remember, working can be a key to your personal fulfillment and how you can make a real difference and contribution. It's also a very important avenue for you to save more for your retirement. Remember to listen to your parents' voices when they said, "Go get a job!"

CHAPTER SEVEN

Do I Have to Worry About Saving for Retirement if I Have a Pension Plan/a Husband/My House Is Paid Off? (Or Any Other Excuses You Can Come Up With!)

To have the retirement you know you want, make sure to save and invest for yourself without excuses!

The truth of the matter is many women don't have any of their own money saved for retirement, or have not been paying attention to what their husbands have been doing with their retirement savings. They have all kinds of excuses for not having saved—and to be fair, some are reasonable. Yet, they all want to retire and often have grand plans for what they will be doing in retirement. For Baby Boomer women, the model for retirement will be different from previous generations, which will require women be more engaged and prepared to handle the financial side of retirement. They cannot stick their heads in the sand and stay detached from their finances. Odds are high that women will eventually live alone and therefore have to manage their finances for some or all of their retirement.

It can be challenging to get involved with retirement finances if you were on one path, and then it takes a sudden turn. For example, one woman got divorced, but managed to put all five of her children through college—an impressive accomplishment. Her concern is that she doesn't own a house and doesn't know how she can afford the rent for the rest of her life. She lives in an area where there is no rent control and wants to stay close to her family and life-long friends. Another woman was married to a physician. She was a homemaker and raised their three children. She had a wonderful life. After the kids left the nest, the marriage fizzled. She realized too late that she had no savings or assets in her name. Another woman planned to use her house as her retirement income. It had appreciated in value tremendously in the 30 years since she bought it and the mortgage was paid off, but when asked where she was going to live once she sold it, she looked startled. She was thinking about the financial windfall, not that she would have to pay today's prices for a new place to live. That nest egg she was counting on was now about 75% smaller than she realized.

Four Components of Money Management

The bottom line is that you are in very good company if you haven't thought about building your own sizeable nest egg that you direct and control. It's just not something many married women thought about over the years. As noted in an earlier chapter, women are skilled in managing cash—working the family budget, making ends meet. But there are four components of money management, not just one or two. It is important that you actively participate in all four areas and understand how you and your spouse or partner will work together to create income for your retirement. It doesn't matter if you haven't done this before. You can get started by taking the reins today!

- First, there's **earning it**, whether that means you had a career outside the home or inside the home. At-home moms work harder than everyone else and only get "paid" in hugs and kisses.

- Then, there's **spending it**. We've got that covered to a T!

- The next component is **saving it**. This is challenging if you don't have a lot of disposable income or if you didn't learn to save from an early age. Yet, you have to build a foundation of assets before the money can grow.

- Last, but definitely not least, is **investing it**. This is a completely different subject than saving, as you read earlier. It is generally not intuitive, but it is absolutely achievable.

Each of the four components requires a completely different set of skills and discipline. How you earn your money is radically different from how you spend it, and entirely too often, women think that saving and investing are the same thing. These are completely different aspects to retirement finances but closely aligned. You need to have something saved before you can invest.

When it comes to getting yourself ready for retirement, you simply cannot rely solely on your husband or partner or house to hope that you'll have enough. You cannot depend only on a pension plan from your employer. Social Security will not pay all the bills. Learning the skills to both save and invest are critical.

Saving It

Women have earning power like never before, and with earning power comes the potential for wealth building. Our grandmothers were adept at tucking their savings away in tin coffee cans in the back of the cupboard. They pinched pennies and shopped for sale items so that they could put a little bit away for a rainy day. Our moms saved with coupons and S & H green stamps at the grocery store. Kids who had an allowance were often encouraged to save for something special.

That discipline to park some money into a savings account was generally learned at home. Today, even those who know how important it is to save are finding it increasingly difficult to save for retirement. The personal savings rate in the US today is less than 5%. Compare that to the prior 50 years (from 1950 to 2000): the average personal savings rate was 9.8%.[14] Most financial experts agree that each of us needs to save between 10% and 15% of our income (depending on your age) to build a sufficient retirement nest egg.

Retirement Savings Are Falling Short

Women often find themselves behind in their saving for retirement. Many worked in lower paying jobs, choosing careers that had more flexibility but lower pay, or they stepped out of the workforce to raise a family or care for an aging parent. Now, as they near retirement, their savings are low. The good news, however, is that more women now have the opportunity to save for retirement in tax-favored retirement accounts through their employers. The bad news is that not enough women are taking advantage of this opportunity to save aggressively for retirement. The Department of Labor tracks who is saving for retirement through plans at work. They report that of the 62 million women under age 65 working in the US, less than half (only 45%) are participating in their employer's retirement savings plan. This is a double-loss for working women. They are falling well short of saving enough for retirement and are losing out on any matching money from their employer. The bottom line is that too many women are jeopardizing their future retirement income.

Furthermore, many women work in jobs where there is the promise of a pension plan. You should be cautious about these old-fashioned plans and the ability of the organization to pay you a promised amount over a long retirement. The reality is that many pension plans have frozen or shut down entirely. Many more will fall by the wayside during the next several decades, likely even ones run by state governments. The reality is that the majority of pension plans cannot support the number of pensioners they have. Taxpayers are balking at having to support state and local pensions when their schools and roads and parks and infrastructures are crumbling.

Look realistically at the potential that you could lose some or all of your pension income during your retirement years and plan for that possibility. You may receive a "cash balance"—a specific dollar amount used to fund your future retirement monthly payments—if the plan is terminated. However, you are then responsible for investing and managing that cash to create some of your income in retirement.

I Need the Money Today

So, why aren't women saving more? The problem with saving for retirement is that there is no immediate reward. At least not for many decades into the future. Trying to save for a retirement that seems 100 years away often gets moved to the back burner when there are so many other family needs today. If you think that saving has no reward that's likely because you get nothing tangible in a shopping bag. Instead, you "spend" that money by putting it in a savings account and then what? Nothing! It's important to differentiate this money as your "investing money" and it is not meant to have any sort of immediate or tangible prize.

Money that you save has only two purposes:

1) Protection for you and your family in case of an emergency, or

2) Growth and compounding for future goals.

That's it. The savings you put aside is strictly intended for security or growth not for today's shoes or groceries. Your emergency fund provides protection if you lose your job, have an unexpected expenditure or hit a financial roadblock. The other money you set aside needs to grow to meet your future retirement. Remember that you'll have to create a paycheck on your own once your employer paycheck stops.

Investing It

Once you have built up a few hundred or thousand dollars, how do you get started investing for growth? After all, if you are going to give up something you really wanted, you may as well make sure you are doing everything possible to grow a big haystack of more money. You've heard the phrase "the rich get richer." It's true. It's because those with money use what they have saved to double and triple in value by investing. That's how compounding works: Choose the right investments and over time your money will grow from say $3,000 to $6,000 to $12,000 to $24,000. There's a catch: when you invest, you could lose some or all of your money, and that is a scary prospect for many women.

Have you ever found money in a parking lot or on the sidewalk? You might feel like it's your lucky day. No one is around who could have dropped it, so now it's yours. That's how we feel when we invest our money and it is growing. Your investments are on the upswing, when the market is doing well, but what if you were the person who dropped the money? You probably would feel disappointed. That's how you'll feel when your investments lose value in a bad market cycle.

We need to get beyond that bad feeling. Investing is a gamble, a game, a bet on the odds. There is risk involved. It is your hard earned money at stake, but the bottom line is that the money you've saved can only grow if you learn to play in the investment market. Your money cannot and will not grow just because you want it to. Women tend to shy away from investing because they don't understand the game or feel uncomfortable putting their money at risk. To the contrary, women are quite adept at investing and have the discipline to be good investors.

Learn to love the investing game:

Ladies, there are lots of games we don't really understand but we are fans anyway. Are you a baseball fan? When was the last time you hit a 98 mile per hour pitch? Do you love football? And yet, have you ever caught a 50-yard pass or tackled a 225 pound running back? Just because we haven't played on the diamond or the gridiron doesn't mean we haven't learned the rules.

From a recent Washington Post story: women make up an estimated 45% of the National Football League fan base. That's about 67 million of us! Women have been tagged as the NFL's most valuable players. Why? Because we buy so much football stuff and influence the buying decisions from the sponsors who run commercials during the games!

Maybe it took a while for you to enjoy these games. Perhaps you like the social parts of game day or an evening out at the ball field. Or best yet, you loved watching your kids play hockey, soccer, tennis, volleyball and ultimate Frisbee, cheering them on for years. We've learned to love sports.

We need to do the same thing for investing. We need to learn to love it.

Don't Abdicate—Participate!

There are several steps you should take to get comfortable learning to invest. It will take time and patience, but stick with it and use your resources. Over time you will become more and more proficient and confident. Even if you would rather work with a professional financial advisor, you still can't abdicate your involvement in investing. You need to have a basic understanding of investing principles so that you know your advisors are doing right by you and choosing specific investments that you are comfortable with. Here are several ways to get into the game of investing:

- **Magazines.** Choose a good, general financial magazine to subscribe to. You want a good resource to start learning from, but make it in a format that you're likely to use. Subscribe to *Money* or *Kiplinger's* along with *People* and *Vanity Fair*! Once you reach age 50, you can get AARP's magazine focused on retirement topics.

- **Online.** Find three good online resources that you'll use to learn about investing. Some suggestions include Motley Fool, Investopedia, and AAII—the American Association of Individual Investors. Many of the mutual fund company websites (such as Vanguard, Fidelity, and T Rowe Price, among others) have a wealth of information about learning to invest—from articles to videos and online apps.

- **Investment Company.** Choose one primary financial investment company. There are many options out there, so do your homework if you don't already have one. Look for rock-solid financial firms that have comprehensive websites with tools, educational information and round-the-clock phone representatives who are willing to answer all of your questions without making you feel uncomfortable or inadequate. Investment companies like Fidelity, Vanguard, Schwab, and T Rowe Price are excellent places to start your research. See how well you can navigate their websites and if you can find the information you are looking for quickly. Make sure the information is written in such a way that you can understand and build on what you are learning.

- **Education.** You may find it more helpful to attend online educational web seminars or in-person presentations. Most of the largest financial firms and banks and insurance companies offer such educational events for free. Take advantage of them and start to learn the language of investing. Look for ones that are free and that you can replay as needed.

- **Newspapers.** Subscribe to the *Wall St. Journal*. In the land of investing, there really is no better way to learn about various investment topics, economics and finance than to read. As you become more comfortable with investment topics, the Journal is a must-have resource. Choose the print version or digital version for your tablet. The key is to get into the habit of reading several articles every day and before long, you'll have a good handle on the language.

- **Your Employer.** Find out what resources your employer (or your spouse's or partner's employer) has to offer along with the retirement plan. Most employers who offer a 401(k), 403(b), or 457 also have a treasure trove of educational resources available to their employees. Talk to your benefits person or Human Resources department if you don't know where to find these resources. It is well worth your time to know what information is already available at no charge to you.

- **Retirement Newsletters.** Subscribe to one of the retirement-specific newsletters that are available. You'll want to understand the retirement landscape as well as investing information for retirement income. MarketWatch's *Retirement Weekly*, *Consumer Reports Money Advisor* and *Kiplinger's Retirement Report* are all excellent choices.

Shopping For the Right Investments

When you start out investing, it can be challenging. How can you choose which investments to buy? Think of it like shopping at a new store that is filled with stocks and bonds and mutual funds. In much the same way we bargain shop for shoes and gifts, we can shop for investments. The problem is that it is just so boring! Glossy magazines and beautiful photos add enjoyment and interest to the process. Who doesn't enjoy flipping through the latest fashion or cooking magazine? We love to watch new products in action on TV's shopping networks and we spend hours engrossed in cooking and baking shows every week. It's just plain fun. We get great ideas and find new ways to show our love to our children, grandchildren, friends and family.

In marked contrast, have you looked at the stock pages of the financial papers? They are often viewed as boring and dry. There are about 5,000 publicly traded stocks, more than

7,700 mutual funds, and thousands of bonds, commodities and other investment instruments to buy. Thousands of lines of symbols and numbers. All in black and white. If you spend time online searching for investments on a variety of financial websites, there is more color and information, but still just charts and graphs and ticker symbols. The descriptions of the investments seem to be in a foreign language.

Unless you have a lot of time (at least one to two hours a day) to spend tracking the broad market trends, the underlying leading and lagging indicators, and the individual companies whose stock you own, you might be better served to stick to mutual funds. Mutual funds are run by investment managers who love to track the market and trade individual stocks and rebalance portfolios. Mutual funds are generally described as a basket of individual stocks. Your money is placed into a "pool" with lots of other folks and the mutual fund managers purchase large blocks of specific stock or bond investments. Your investment is a share of the total mutual fund.

Think of mutual funds as a recipe. Think about a chocolate cake you buy at the bakery. It was made with a number of ingredients in specific measurements. The cake is like a mutual fund. When you buy a mutual fund, there are lots of ingredients (individual company's stock) included in specific measurements (number of shares). The professional mutual fund manager chooses the ingredients and measures them. He or she is the pastry chef. You'll pay a mutual fund fee for his services (just like you pay for that bakery cake), but this way you only have to keep track of a few mutual fund investments.

Earlier in this chapter, you read about many resources you can use to learn about investing. If you are ready to shop for specific investments, there are a number of important steps to take. You take similar steps when shopping for shoes:

- **Do your homework (choose your store).** Whether stocks or mutual funds or any investment, you need to research the details. Which investment company will you work with? Who is in charge? Do you understand what you are investing in?

- **Assess performance (try them on for fit).** What is the investment's track record? How did it perform during the last recession? What is its best return? How often can the underlying investments change?

- **Evaluate the risk (how much will they hurt?).** How volatile is the investment? Are you comfortable taking on that amount of risk?

- **Understand the fees (is there a sale?).** No investment is free. There are different kinds of fees and prices on mutual funds and commissions or transaction fees for trading individual stocks. Know what you are paying and if you can get it less expensive somewhere else.

Getting in the investment game is an important step. Even if you've owned mutual funds in your retirement account for years, have you looked at them lately? How are they performing? Do you have the best mix of stocks and bonds in your account as you approach retirement? Might it be time to make a change?

You can't excuse yourself from investing even if it's boring:

One of the reasons women are so disengaged in investing is simply because there is nothing interesting to grab our attention. We have to exchange our valuable time from the other hundreds of daily obligations we already have on our plate to turn around and study the investment pages of the financial papers. The information is valuable and in a much-needed shorthand, if you are part of the investment "club". Getting to that point is arduous if you don't naturally love investments and the whole drama and excitement found on Wall Street's stock trading floor.

However, that doesn't mean you can excuse yourself from investing. It just means you need to find a way to get some level of understanding of the concepts and find a method of investing that works for you. If you aren't married to an investment guy, you probably need to find one or become an expert yourself. Search the Financial Planning website (www.plannersearch.org) for local advisors who focus on planning and investing for retirement. Check out the Retirement Income Industry Association (www.riia-usa.org) for a list of advisors who specialize in helping people create income for retirement.

CHAPTER EIGHT

Should I Take Social Security at 62?

In short, no.

Unless you are incredibly wealthy, it is highly likely that the income you receive from Social Security will be the most important income source you have throughout your retirement and old age. Women are especially dependent on Social Security as they live longer in retirement. You will be well-served to plan for a long retirement, spanning two or three decades or longer. You may become a widow and lose some income that was coming in from your spouse's resources. You'll need to have an income source that you know you can rely on. According to the Social Security Administration, about 56% of Social Security recipients are women over 62; 67% are women over the age of 85. While you can't predict your future with any certainty, you can certainly plan for having income throughout your retirement.

Social Security is a complex government program that is often misunderstood. At the core of the retirement program, it provides a small foundation of income throughout retirement to keep former workers and their spouses out of poverty. The key word here is "small." It was never designed or intended to be a replacement for your working paycheck, but many think it is. Because of this, when they look at how little of their income it will replace, they are surprised.

A Brief Overview

A few important points about how Social Security works:

- There are two types of Social Security benefits: the retirement program and the disability insurance program. They are separate trust funds that operate with different purposes.

- The retirement program is for retired workers and their spouses. Workers and their employers each contribute to the retirement program. Certain public institutions, state governments and unions may not pay into Social Security, but rather, provide a pension for their retired workers. Therefore these employees are not eligible for Social Security benefits on their own work history.

- The program tries to accommodate every type of situation you can imagine, so it can seem unduly complicated. For example, Social Security addresses you as an individual worker, as well as you as a spouse. It allows for early access to your benefits if you become a widow. Married couples have several ways to maximize benefits in collaboration with each other (including same-sex married couples, but check the details for your state with the Social Security Administration).

All in all, there are hundreds of different outcomes that are possibilities for your Social Security payment. Once you've made your decision, you've locked in this key source of income for as long as you live.

Why is age 62 important and why do we all know about it?

Understanding your benefit and figuring out your options well before your 62nd birthday is of utmost importance.

For all that we don't know and understand about investing, finance, longevity and taxes, it is amazing that most women know with certainty that the earliest age they can take their Social Security benefit is 62. Let's face it, by our mid-50's we're getting pretty tired. We've been working and raising children, running a household and making a difference in our communities and families for 30 some-odd years. We've hit menopause after a rocky journey. We've dealt with our children flying the coop, and sometimes returning as adults. Our careers have been up and down. Through it all, we have persevered and prospered with a positive perspective. Now, we are ready to complete this leg of our marathon and slow things down a little. Knowing that we can replace some income with our well-earned Social Security benefits at 62 seems like a pretty good idea. Not to mention that many women—and men, as well—think they won't get their fair due if they don't jump into the pool as soon as possible.

If you take nothing else from this book, please understand that if you claim your Social Security retirement benefit at 62, or at any time before reaching your full retirement age, you are locking in a permanent and significant penalty. Your income from Social Security in retirement and throughout your old age will be permanently reduced.

Find Your Social Security Statement Today

Before you even think about filing that claim for benefits starting at 62 (or any other age), have you done the math? When thinking about the viability of your long-term retirement income, your Social Security decision is just about the most important one you will make. It is a major financial decision that will have far-reaching and long-lasting implications on your retirement finances in your old age. Think about how important this payment will be when you're 87 or 92 or 96. It's not just for income in your 60s and 70s.

Spending time on Social Security's website will be well worth the effort. Start by finding your Social Security statement. You may have received a copy in the mail or go to www.ssa.gov and sign up under the "*my Social Security*" tab to access your most current statement. There are many factors to consider before you make your decision to claim and this statement gives you the best information on your work record and your calculated Social Security estimated amounts. What you'll find on your statement:

- **Eligibility.** Are you eligible for Social Security retirement benefits? Your statement tells you if you have qualified for retirement benefits. You must reach age 62 and have earned 40 credits, which are based on wages. You earn up to four (4) credits per year, and can do so by working for 10 years in a row or by accumulating credits over many years as you've moved in and out of employment. It doesn't matter when you earn the credits; you just need 40 to qualify.

- **Full Retirement Age.** Social Security calculates your retirement benefit that aligns with your "full retirement age" or FRA. Your FRA corresponds to a specific birth year. If you were born in 1960 or later, your FRA is 67. If you were born between 1943 and 1959, your full retirement age is 66 and some number of months. Everyone used to have an FRA of 65, but it was changed under the *Social Security Amendments of 1983*. Why is your FRA important? Social Security locks in the age when you should begin receiving your retirement benefit and calculates your estimate at FRA. If you tap Social Security before your FRA, you are penalized permanently. If you wait longer, you get a bonus.

- **Highest 35 years of earnings.** Your benefit is calculated based on your highest 35 years of earnings. Take a look at your work record—do you even have 35 years of work history yet? At age 55, you may be surprised to see that you might not have worked 35 years. What if you stepped out of the workforce for 8 years to stay home with your children? There is a gap in your record for those years on your earnings history. Any zero dollar years will be included in your calculation if you don't replace them with earnings.

Adjustments to Your Retirement Benefits

Before you decide you are going to claim this very important income benefit as your 62nd birthday present to yourself, see if you have even met the basics for getting your highest calculated value. If not, your actual payment may be lower than it should be because you didn't optimize your work history and make adjustments while you still had time. Other adjustments will be made to your actual Social Security payment based on your personal facts and circumstances:

- If you claim before FRA and at the earliest age of 62, the penalty results in a permanent reduction in your benefit of up to 25% or 30%. That is a huge reduction in your retirement salary every year.

- If you can wait to claim your benefit until after your full retirement age, there is a built in "bonus". Your income will be increased by 8% per year that you delay. There is a special calculation that applies "delayed retirement credits" to your benefit between your FRA and age 70.

- Once you reach age 65 and enroll in Medicare, your Social Security payment is automatically reduced to pay your Medicare Part B premium.

- If you decide to claim Social Security before your FRA and continue to work, you may get a temporarily reduced payment. There are earnings thresholds that you cannot exceed if you are going to "double dip" by working and drawing early Social Security. The dollar amounts are quite low and change each year, so check the Social Security website for the most current information.

- Your Social Security income may also be taxable based on your other income for the year. Many people will have at least a portion of their benefit taxed.

- If you have certain state or government pensions in addition to qualifying for Social Security, the Windfall Elimination Provision (WEP) and the Government Pension Offset (GPO) will reduce your Social Security benefits. If this is your situation, find detailed information and calculators on the Social Security website.

Outliving the Averages

How long you may live is also a key factor when you are thinking about your Social Security benefit. We know that a man reaching age 65 today can expect to live, on average, until age 84, but a woman can expect to almost reach age 87.[22] The most current actuary tables show that the average life expectancy for each has increased about 2 years. Ladies, that means on average, you can expect to live to age 89.[23] And those are just averages. About one out of every four 65-year-old women will live past age 90, and one in 10 will live past age 95.

Thinking about how long you could live translates to how long you will need an income. If you begin your Social Security payments at 62, those payments need to stretch out for 30 or 35 years or longer. If you wait until your full retirement age of 66+ or 67, your monthly income is higher because it will be paid over fewer years. If you can wait until age 70 to claim, your monthly income increase is sizeable.

Married Women and Claiming Social Security—It's Complicated

Many married women find themselves in the situation where they have a low (or no) earnings record. Their spouse was the breadwinner in the family. If you are in this situation, you are still entitled to a Social Security benefit under the "spousal beneficiary" rules. As a spouse (or ex-spouse), you are entitled to up to half of your husband's Social Security benefit.

If you become a widow (including when your ex-spouse dies), you may be entitled to survivor benefits based on your deceased spouse's benefit. Assuming he was the higher earner, you would step into his shoes and receive his Social Security benefit payment.

Here's a simple example of how your spousal benefits might work:

Higher-Earning Spouse	Lower-Earning Spouse	Your Household Benefit is combined	If the Higher-Earning Spouse Dies first...
If his Social Security FRA benefit is **$2,000/mo**...	...your spousal benefit at your FRA is **$1,000/mo** (50% of his benefit)	**$3,000/mo** while both of you are alive	...you "step into his shoes" and will receive **$2,000/mo** in survivor benefits, reducing your overall household income

Social Security is complicated. There are many factors to consider before deciding when you and your spouse should claim your benefits. It gets more complicated when both spouses have work records and you have to coordinate claiming strategies for optimal benefits. The Social Security Administration will calculate if you will be better off using your spouse's (or ex-spouse's) earnings record or your own. In any case, claiming before your full retirement age will reduce your benefit permanently.

More Complications (and Opportunities) for Married Couples

There are additional options available for married couples to consider. Certain combinations of claiming strategies can help you maximize your income. There are several options you'll want to explore if you are married:

1. **Coordinated timing.** You'll need to determine who will be tapping their Social Security benefit first, at what age, and who might maximize the benefit. How does your timing for collecting Social Security coincide with your decision to retire versus your husband's retirement date?

2. **The "claim and suspend" option.** This option allows the higher earning spouse to file for Social Security at full retirement age, but "suspend" collecting payments until later. This opens up the *spousal benefit* for the lower-earning spouse and allows her or him to collect up to 50% of the higher earning spouse's calculated benefit.

3. **The "claim now, claim more later" option.** In this option, after reaching full retirement age, one spouse starts collecting their *spousal benefit* (up to 50% of the spouse's full benefit amount) while both spouses continue to leave their individual benefits alone until age 70. When each reaches age 70, each of their benefits has increased 8% per year in "delayed

retirement credits"—an extra "bonus." At that time the spouse collecting the spousal benefit switches to collecting on their own record and the spouse who delayed collecting begins receiving Social Security income.

Figuring out how to optimize your Social Security or to maximize it, when to start collecting and on whose work record is complex. Since your decision is all but irrevocable, it is of utmost importance that you get it right—well before you file an application for your benefits and well before you actually claim.

In light of this information, let's look at the question that opened this chapter: "Should I take Social Security at 62?" The answer may not be so easy to come up with, but it's critically important that you take the time to figure out the claiming strategy that will work best for your retirement and to protect yourself and your spouse for the future.

Excellent Social Security Resources:

Getting your arms around the complexities of Social Security is no simple task, especially for married couples. Start reading up on your options well before you have decisions to make. There are some particularly good resources available for your use:

- Dana Anspach is a retirement financial advisor, CFP® and RMA® who writes a terrific retirement column on About.com. Check out her Social Security information at http://moneyover55.about.com/

- For a book that gets into more of the technical rules of Social Security in an understandable way, read *Get What's Yours, The Secrets to Maxing Out Your Social Security* By Laurence J. Kotlikoff, Philip Moeller and Paul Solman

- Kiplinger's website has an excellent section on Social Security that is worth your time to explore under the "retirement" tab on www.kiplinger.com

- You can find links to some very good Social Security calculators at boomerretirementbriefs.com, or use the calculators on the Social Security website for more basic information on your own work record or for a spousal benefit.

CHAPTER NINE

Can I Really Live to 100?

Of the 80,000 centenarians in the US today, over 80% are women.

A 67-year old woman who retired to Florida nine years ago was talking about how great it is to live in Florida. She was from New England originally and lived up north in snow country all her life. Since her move she celebrates every afternoon under a Tiki hut with a margarita. She is very active, enjoying water aerobics, long walks, and swing dancing at least four nights a week. The weather is wonderful 10 months out of the year (she goes back to New England in July and August) and there is no shortage of things to do. There is just a shortage of men! As a single woman (divorced a few years ago), dating was on her list. According to her observations, among those over age 65, there are eight women to every one man in Florida. While her numbers may be a little off, it may surely seem that men are a rare sighting in the active groups of aging Floridians.

Population Realities

Women eventually become the super-majority of the population. Overall population in the United States is split about

50/50 between males and females (49.2% males and 50.8% females) in 2013. By about age 55, a shift begins to occur where women make up a larger percentage of the population. By the time we reach the traditional retirement age of 65, there is a significant shift underway:[15]

Age	% male	% female
65 to 69 years	47.3%	52.7%
70 to 74 years	46.0%	54.0%
75 to 79 years	44.2%	55.8%
80 to 84 years	41.1%	58.9%
85 years and over	33.8%	66.2%

The percentage of females increases from about 53% when entering retirement to two-thirds at the end of retirement. On average, women live longer than men. Sometimes, a lot longer. That means our retirement will, on average, be longer.

Living into Old Age

The single biggest factor when considering your own retirement is how long you might live. You may be one of the women who live well into your 90s or even reach 100. The problem when planning for retirement is that none of us has a crystal ball that tells us how long we'll live. Since we won't know until it's too late, we must plan for our money to last a long time in retirement, but for how long? Ideally, you'll want to plan that your retirement will last into your mid-90s. If you have longevity in your family, you should plan for even longer. If you have some significant health issues, you may decide to plan for a shorter time. But, think positively. 70 is the new 50!

Take a look at the changing face of American women everywhere you turn. Look at your own family and friends.

Is your mom, your grandmother or an aunt alive into their 90s? Are your friends' moms alive into their 90s? How many birthday parties have you hosted or attended for relatives who reached various milestones of 90, 95, or 100-plus? It's more than you might think at first glance. Realize that these older women have already spent some 30 to 35 years in retirement. That's the span or the "retirement horizon" that you'll need to plan for as well.

Why the female of most animal species lives longer is unknown, but there are some interesting hypotheses. Some researchers think it might be because women are more social, which can reduce stress and keep a network available when we are in trouble. A more scientific theory focuses on how the "length of our lives is regulated by the balance between how fast new damage strikes our cells and how efficiently this damage is corrected."[16] From a biological view, our bodies age due to the "gradual buildup of a huge number of individually tiny faults" in the cellular working of our insides. Another theory, biologically speaking: "Could it be that women live longer because they are less disposable than men?" This gets back to the practical realities of survival of a species and that the female is needed to give birth to the offspring and feed them. Regardless of why women live longer, we need to make sure to prepare for a long life and the fact that we may eventually be on our own.

If you are still not convinced that you need to plan for a long retirement, take a look at these facts about the reality of living to an old age:[17]

- In 2010, there were 40 million people age 65 and over living in the United States—13% of the total population. To put this in perspective, there were only 3 million citizens over the age of 65 in 1900.[18]

- The 65+ population is projected to grow rapidly, more than doubling from 35 million in 2000 to 72 million in 2030. This older group will represent nearly 20% of the total U.S. population.

- The oldest of our population (age 85 and over) grew from just over 100,000 in 1900 to 720,000 in 1980 and to 5.5 million in 2010. This group is expected to reach at least 19 million by 2050. Some researchers predict that death rates at older ages will decline more rapidly than is reflected in this estimate due to medical advances. That would lead to even faster growth of the aged population.[19]

We know that women will make up the lion's share of this aging population. Are you surprised to learn that women aged 90 and older outnumber men who are 90+ nearly 3 to 1? Over 80% of women who reach age 90+ are widowed, while more than 40 percent of the 90+ men are married.[20]

Back to the original question of this chapter: Can I really live to 100? Yes, you really can. The United States currently has the largest number of known centenarians of any nation with 53,364 according to the 2010 Census. In 2010, 82.8% of US centenarians were female.[21]

The next question you'll need to answer is: Will my retirement finances last if I live to 100?

Celebrating with 100 candles

Remember back in 1983 when the Today Show started announcing the names of those Americans who reached age 100? Back then, it was quite rare for someone to reach 100.

Today, it is much more common. Check your own local newspapers for centenarian celebrations. One headline read, "Getting Old is Not for Wimps!" from a woman turning 100. Another read, "Three centenarian sisters reunite" where the youngest sister is 102, the middle is 104 and the oldest just turned 110. They got together to celebrate the eldest's 110th birthday. A company located in a small New England town, Vita Needle, has an average working age of 74. It is not uncommon for an employee there to celebrate a 100th birthday. (For a fascinating look at this intriguing business read Caitrin Lynch's book, *Retirement on the Line: Age, Work, and Value in an American Factory.*)

Retirement communities and nursing homes are teeming with aged women. We have to be very realistic about our chances of living to old, old age. Ladies, our chances are very good.

CHAPTER TEN

Where Do I Fit Retirement Planning into My Jam-Packed Days? I'm Already Too Busy.

Between Facebook and dinner!

Regardless of their path in life, there is no woman who has spare time in her day. It just doesn't happen. How often have we heard, "Well, if you want something done, give it to a busy woman?" It's a nod to women's incredible ability to get things organized and done.

The reality is that most women are too busy to even add the critical function of investor to their plates. We covered how women are the CEO of the family, and generally not the Chief Investment Officer. The structure of a woman's day is complicated. From tending and nurturing the children and managing the house to entertaining guests and supporting her spouse or partner, she is on the go. And, that's after putting in a full day on the job.

Dreading Dinner

By far, she handles daily meal preparation. According to the National Institutes of Health tracking of time spent cooking, women spend 66 minutes per day making meals. Once you add in the planning, the grocery shopping and the clean-up, it's more likely to average about 2 hours per day. The good news is that today's woman spends a lot less time in the kitchen. Our moms back in 1965 spent about 113 minutes a day just preparing meals!

Why bring up dinner when we're talking about retirement planning? Women who are 55 have now made or arranged for about 12,000 dinners, plus 12,000 lunches, and 12,000 breakfasts. An enormous amount of time goes into feeding the family. It is one of the three most basic necessities we need to live. There is no question that we need to eat…and someone needs to cook, but it takes such a large chunk of time out of the productive day that other things can't be done. Assuming you will live another 33 years, you will spend another 24,000 hours in your kitchen preparing and cooking another 36,000 meals. Imagine what you could do if you replaced these two hours each day to think about planning for your retirement!

Lost Online

It's easy to get lost during the day on social media sites. Women thrive on being connected and staying connected, on sharing updates and good deals. Shockingly, we are spending an enormous amount of time in front of our computers "socializing" virtually. A recent study shows that we are spending nearly 3 hours each day on smartphones![24] That is a lot of screen time. We still spend, on average, some 2 hours and 48 minutes a day watching TV.

The point? There are some hours in each of our days that we could redirect to learning more about investing, planning more realistically for retirement, and having the conversations with our spouses, partners, friends, or grown children about how we want to spend our next chapter.

Finding Time for Retirement Finances

Even though women typically bear the burden of managing the family, we can't ignore the need to be involved in our own plans for retirement and the financial resources we'll need. It can be challenging and often overwhelming. Find a way to redirect some of your time and money to make sure you feel prepared when it's your turn to retire. Maybe find an occasional hour or two each week after dinner but before Facebook.

Here are a few ideas that other women have shared that are working for them. One of these might work for you:

- **The tax-time review**—No one loves the intrusion that tax season brings each year. You just get through a hectic two months of holiday stress and fun, you're getting the house put back together, and those pesky tax documents start to arrive. Some women have embraced tax season as the time of year to do their retirement planning. Since all of their statements are readily available, they have found it easier and less of a burden to deal with all of their financial planning at once. February and March is the time they pull together their tax information, do a detailed review of their retirement financial situation, and make any decisions they need to implement for the New Year.

- **The back porch weekend**—Another woman was having a hard time finding enough quality time for in-depth conversations about retirement with her husband. With both of them working full-time, kids at home, and lots of other activities and obligations, there was just not enough time to talk. Every time one of them wanted to discuss retirement life or retirement finances, the conversation quickly dissolved into an argument. One summer, the kids were at camp and they found themselves home alone over the long July 4th weekend. It turned out to be the perfect weekend to sit on the back porch, enjoy the long warm days and have that in-depth conversation about what they each were thinking about retirement. That weekend was so successful that they have made it their annual "let's plan for our retirement" weekend.

- **The quarterly snapshot**—Some women, especially those getting closer to retirement prefer to look at their financials more than once a year. They tend to check quickly each month when their statements arrive, but do a more in-depth review about once each quarter. They are making decisions about their investments and if there are any changes they want to make. Looking at their whole picture more frequently helps them feel more in control of their retirement finances.

- **Bills and balances**—Still others like to stay right on top of their investments, so they do a monthly review at the same time they pay their bills. They tend to set aside one or two evenings a month to pay bills and review their various savings accounts and retirement investment accounts.

- **Trusting my husband**—You may be one of the many married women who has not been very involved in investments during your marriage. Your husband is comfortable with investing and you are happy that he is so involved. You trust him and this arrangement has worked well for you. Now it's time to get more involved. If something were to happen to your husband, you will need to know where all your money is. You'll need access to all of the investment accounts. You need to know how they will be passed on to you. You don't have to become an investment guru, but you do need to ensure that you are financially protected.

There is no need to go it alone with all of these retirement financial matters. Even if you want to self-manage all your money, it's still a good idea to work with professionals. You'll find most major financial services companies have knowledgeable representatives when you call their 800 number or walk into a branch office. There are many flavors of financial planners and advisors who might be helpful to you. Check the professional associations of financial advisors to get an idea of what services they provide and how they get paid.

The bottom line is it's important that you decide how involved you want to be. The less involved you are, the more trusted professional advisors you'll need in your court. There are many excellent advisors and resources out there, and you need to find the ones that will work with you.

You can find a list of resources for finding advisors on boomerretirementbriefs.com.

Finding the Right Advisors

Surrounding yourself with the right team of advisors can take some time. Interview a range of professionals and make sure you can really talk to them and that they answer your questions in a way you can understand. As you approach retirement, your advisors need to be expert and savvy about retirement topics. Most of us need several advisors on our retirement team:

1. **A financial planner and advisor** who also specializes in preparing clients for retirement and is an expert in Social Security and Medicare.

2. **An estate planning attorney** who can help you set up your financial house so that your assets and property pass down the way you want them to. He or she also helps you with your health care proxy and other important considerations that you need to address as you age.

3. **An executor** (person and/or institution) to manage how you want your property handled.

4. **A tax accountant** who is an expert in retirement account distributions. Different tax-advantaged accounts have different tax rules, plus some of your Social Security benefit may be taxable.

See the "Resources" section for a list of websites to start your search.

Parting Words

No more excuses. Getting ready to retire is a big deal. And odds are good that you are not prepared well enough for the financial realities of retirement. Focus on building your confidence and knowledge about your retirement. You took an important step by reading this book. You are now more ready than ever to get started planning for your own retirement or continuing to build your plans.

Remember, it will take longer than a weekend to get your plan in place. You're still running that marathon of your life. You may have a lot of miles behind you, but you still have a lot of miles in front of you, too. The odds are in your favor to live for a long time, so enjoy the journey.

Get started today. Until you can answer the question "How much money will I need for my retirement?" you've got some work to do. Now that you have an outline and some resources all in one place, you are ready to go!

Good luck! Let me hear how you are doing.

You can contact me through Facebook (BoomerRetirementBriefs) or Twitter (@MarciaMantell).

Resources

Through the chapters of the book there were various resources that every woman can use to better prepare for retirement. Here is the complete list by chapter.

Chapter 1: My blog www.BoomerRetirementBriefs.com showcases ideas about retirement from Boomers who have embraced this period of their lives. A fun blog about life after kids is www.gypsynesters.com

Chapter 2: www.Amazon.com where you can search for finance, retirement and investing books (while shopping for gifts and shoes!) A few favorites: *On My Own Two Feet* by Manisha Thakor and Sharon Kedar and *An Optimists Guide to Retirement: Looking Forward* by Ellen Freudenheim. Use the retirement income planning tools on www.Fidelity.com and www.TRowePrice.com to see your numbers

Chapter 3: IRAs can be set up at most financial firms. Check the websites at companies such as Fidelity Investments, Vanguard, Schwab, T Rowe Price, Wells Fargo, Bank of America or any financial firm you are familiar with

Chapter 4: www.KhanAcademy.org and www. BetterMoneyHabits.com

Chapter 5: A budget worksheet that includes categories for how women prioritize and spend their money at www. BoomerRetirementBriefs.com

Chapter 6: Your employer—talk to your HR or benefits department about all your retirement options. Make adjustments as needed to shore up your retirement savings. Also, get your Social Security statement at www.SSA.gov

Chapter 7: If you have a pension, get the plan document and read it. Find out your options. If you own a home, find your current mortgage statement and figure out how much you still owe.

Chapter 8: www.SSA.gov, www.SSA.gov, www.SSA. gov—it's just that important! And, refer back to Chapter 8, page 85, for additional resources

Chapter 9: Refer back to pages 69–71 for many investment and financial resources and tips. For an excellent look at working at older ages, read Caitrin Lynch's *Retirement on the Line: Age, Work, and Value in an American Factory*

Chapter 10: www.RIIA-USA.org has a list of advisors who hold the Retirement Management Analyst® designation; to find a Certified Financial Planner® in your state, www. OneFPA.org; to find a fee-only financial planner, www. NAPFA.org

Check the American Institute of CPA's website to find accountants in your area (www.aicpa.org).

Ask friends, family or your financial advisor for referrals to Estate Planning attorneys and read *What's the Deal with Estate Planning?* by Peggy R. Hoyt.

Endnotes

1. New York Life, "Loss of a Spouse" study, 2014

2. Bankrate.com, survey of Americans, August 2014

3. BlackRock Global Investor Pulse Survey, October 2014

4. Brad Barber and Terrance Odean, University of California, Boys Will Be Boys: Gender, Overconfidence and Common Stock Investment, 2001

5. Vanguard Investment Research study of 2.7 million IRA owners and their trading activity, published 2010

6. GAO analysis of Federal Reserve Survey of Consumer Finances, 2010 data

7. Daily Mail Reporter, "A Nation of Shoe Addicts?" 5/15/2014 (this is a terrifically fun article to read!)

8. Fidelity Investments Viewpoint, January 2014. https://www.fidelity.com/viewpoints/retirement/8X-retirement-savings

9. Hewitt, The Real Deal 2008 Study, published June 2008

10. Author's calculations assuming monthly investments and 5% return rate, net of inflation. For illustration only.

11. Department of Labor and Bureau of Labor Statistics for 2014

12. American Association of University Women (AAUW), The Simple Truth about the Gender Pay Gap (Spring 2015)

13. US News, http://money.usnews.com/money/blogs/planning-to-retire/2011/08/17/average-retirement-age-grows

14. Bureau of Economic Analysis, National Income and Product Account Tables, Oct 2014, compiled by PGPF

15. 2013 Population Estimates, US Census Bureau - American Fact Finder

16. Scientific American, http://www.scientificamerican.com/article/why-women-live-longer/

17. US Census Bureau, http://www.agingstats.gov/Main_Site/Data/2012_Documents/Population.aspx

18. US Census Bureau, http://www.agingstats.gov/Main_Site/Data/2012_Documents/Population.aspx

19. US Census bureau and Aging Stats: http://www.agingstats.gov/Main_Site/Data/2012_Documents/Population.aspx

20. From NPR and 2010 census: http://www.npr.org/blogs/thetwo-way/2011/11/17/142457598/90-is-the-new-85-oldest-old-population-is-expanding-rapidly

21. US Census Bureau report

22. Social Security based on the 2010 census: http://www.ssa.gov/planners/lifeexpectancy.htm

23. Society of Actuaries, October 2014

24. Bloomberg.com, "We Now Spend More Time Staring at Phones than TVs", Nov 2014

Acknowledgements

Since I was a young girl, I always wanted to write a book. So, it is with much gratitude that I thank Jack Tatar for making my dream a reality. A chance meeting at the Retirement Income Industry Association annual meeting and a conversation about blogs and tweeting were the forerunners to the book idea. Thanks, Jack, for your support and enthusiasm and for welcoming me to your family of "What's the Deal With …"® books.

My heartfelt thanks go out to Polly Walker and Susan Bumstead Chanley for their willingness to always listen to my ideas, put up with my schedule, and offer the most remarkable feedback and edits. Everyone needs a team of people who will challenge their thinking and help build from one idea to the next to deliver a better output. This duo is extraordinary and I am very lucky to call them both friends as well as editors-extraordinaire.

Family is the most important part of my every day. I have two wonderful parents to thank for my financial foundation and for the good advice I shared in Chapter 6. My husband of 32 years and counting has been an exceptional partner and makes every day that much better than the day before. Our retirement should be a blast! Thank you for putting up with me all these years, Dan.

And, thanks go to our two amazing daughters, Katie and Lindsay. They have been such good sports, suffering through years of retirement and financial conversations when they were stuck in the car with us and no DVD player. They are the future, their retirement accounts are growing already and I couldn't be prouder of them.

Meet Marcia Mantell

For nearly 25 years, Marcia Mantell has helped the country's foremost financial services firms and their advisors increase their knowledge of complex retirement concepts and regulations. First at Fidelity Investments, she was Vice President of Retirement, responsible for developing programs to encourage saving in IRAs and Small Business retirement plans. Then, as founder and President of **Mantell Retirement Consulting, Inc.** she partners with financial institutions to help them support their customers across the retirement spectrum—from a focus on saving, to the transition into retirement, to how to organize and manage income to last a lifetime.

Marcia has developed innovative retirement income planning workshops and programs for advisors and their clients, comprehensive retirement education programs and seminars for consumers, and *Money Basics* workshops to help high school students and young adults start out on solid financial footing. She has written extensively about retirement topics. She also has a remarkable ability to translate challenging retirement concepts into everyday language that educates and motivates people to take the right steps to achieve the retirement they desire.

To build successful programs and materials, she pursued an in-depth understanding of how consumers think about retirement and plan (or avoid planning) for the future. She has spent the past two decades talking to Baby Boomers to get a more in-depth view from the inside. Marcia presents to standing room only crowds of consumers who are looking for the "magic answer" to the question that keeps them up at night: Will I really have enough money to last through my retirement?

Marcia interviews Baby Boomers frequently and shares their stories in her blog at **BoomerRetirementBriefs.com**. It offers a light-hearted, but thought-provoking look at how Baby Boomers are reshaping and reinventing retirement. She is often interviewed by the press, including *Consumer Reports Money Advisor, The Wall St. Journal, BankRate, ThinkAdvisor* and was profiled in *Research Magazine.*

She is a graduate of the University of Rochester and holds a Retirement Management Analyst (RMA®) designation. She is an active member of the Retirement Income Industry Association (RIIA), where she heads up Consumer initiatives.

She and her husband raised two daughters in the suburbs of Boston, teaching them from a young age how important it is to save for retirement. She is an active member of her community and serves on several boards.

Marcia would love to hear how you are planning for retirement. You can reach her at BoomerRetirementBriefs. com, on Twitter (@MarciaMantell) or on Facebook (Boomer Retirement Briefs).

Lightning Source UK Ltd.
Milton Keynes UK
UKHW020948291019
352516UK00008B/241/P